The Secret Place

William J. Dupley

THE SECRET PLACE

William J. Dupley

The Secret Place

Copyright © 2011, William J. Dupley

Scripture taken from the HOLY BIBLE, NEW INTERNATIONAL VERSION ®. Copyright © 1973, 1978, 1984 by International Bible Society. Used by permission of Zondervan Publishing House. All rights reserved. • Scripture taken from *The Holy Bible, King James Version.* Copyright © 1977, 1984, Thomas Nelson Inc., Publishers.

ISBN: 978-1-936860-01-2
LSI Edition: 978-1-55452-729-8
E-book ISBN: 978-1-55452-730-4

Cover Painting by Heather Sinnott
www.heathersinnott.com
Artwork by Heather Sinnott and Nancy Young
Back cover and Father & Son photo by Trayc Dudgeon,
www.photosbytrayc.ca

Cataloguing data available from Library and Archives Canada

To order additional copies, visit:
www.essencebookstore.com

For more information, please contact:
Bill Dupley
the.secret.place@rogers.com

Kingdom Heart Publishing
Mississauga, Ontario

Printed in Belleville, Ontario Canada by Essence Publishing.

Dedication

To my wonderful wife, Susan; to my family, who have encouraged me to share my secret place with the Lord; and to Mark Virkler, who taught me how to hear the voice of God.

Contents

Foreword

This book is a forerunner. It shows people how they can have their own secret place with the Lord, enter it daily, and receive wonderful revelation from God. Your stories inspire faith in our hearts, encouraging us to reach out and try the things you have done to discover how they will work in our own lives.

You have torn down the wall between the sacred and the secular and shown how revelation does flow for all of life: healing our hearts, healing our families, personal direction, and assistance at work. And you give us many journaling exercises, which get us started down the right path. Thank you for this contribution to the kingdom of God. Many lives will be touched by it.

Blessings,
Mark Virkler
President of Christian Leadership University
Communion with God Ministries
3792 Broadway St., Buffalo, NY 14227

Acknowledgements

To the people who helped me know my Heavenly Father and without whose help this book would have never been created.

I am grateful for Rev. Fred Fulford, who invested his time and love to teach the word of God. His pastoral care has always been a model to me.

I am thankful for the care and inspiration of Rev. John Arnott, who has taught me my Heavenly Father's heart for me and shown me what grace under fire looks like.

I am thankful for Rev. Steve Long, who has invested a great deal of time to read my journals and help me to me stay on track.

I am thankful for my wife, Sue, and my daughter, Heather, who painstakingly read the first versions of the book and had the courage to tell me it needed work.

I am thankful for my dad who showed me what a father does for the family he loves.

I am very grateful to my sister, Catherine Bowes, who edited every page to ensure it made sense.

I am thankful to Heather Sinnott and Nancy Young for sharing their wonderful artistic gifts to bring to life the images of my secret place.

Introduction

He that dwelleth in the secret place of the most High shall abide under the shadow of the almighty.[1]

This book is an account and description of my secret place with the Lord. It is a true story; it is not fiction. All the details described in this book have happened to me, and I continue to meet with my Heavenly Dad in this place almost every day. I have described the physical attributes of the secret place, the events that have occurred there, and how God has taught me about His character and loving compassion.

Our Heavenly Father talks about a place called the secret place. It is a promise of protection, safety, and communion with God. It is the place where Abraham met God and spoke to him as one man speaks to another. It is the place where every believer can meet God face to face.

Through a series of visions, my Heavenly Father has shown me that this is a very real place. It is a place where we can meet, talk about any topic from business to raising children, and receive specific practical words of wisdom directly from God. We can share our true feelings and fears and develop our relationship with Him. It is a place where our Heavenly Father can father us. The secret place is personal; my secret place will not likely look like someone else's. The secret place is a place where you are comfortable and at ease with your Father.

For many of you, the idea that someone can hear from God every day may be a completely new concept. I was raised in a Christian home and became a Christian when I was 22 years old. For the next 14 years, I faithfully attended church and even went to Bible school, but still I did not know how to hear God.

In 1992, I was invited to a small Vineyard church in Toronto. Here I met Mark Virkler, who promised that I could learn how to hear from God. Mark said God speaks to all His sheep and His sheep know His voice, so if you are not hearing Him consistently, either you are not a sheep or you just don't know how.[2] That was challenging. I knew I was a sheep, so I figured I must just not know how to hear God's voice.

That day Mark introduced us to the ancient biblical method of hearing from God and I did hear God's voice. Over the past 20 years, many people have used this ancient method to hear God's voice. This was the first step on my journey. I could not believe it could be that easy, yet it was, and I will never be the same again.

May this book encourage you to develop your relationship with the Lord and find your own secret place with Him.

Yours,
William Dupley

Personal Action Preparation

This book is designed to help you develop your relationship with the Lord. At the end of each chapter there is a personal action section. These exercises will require you to write down what God says to you. Since these words are often very personal, I recommend that you record what the Lord says to you in a separate notebook that you can review with a trusted friend. This will help you to begin your personal journey in developing a deeper place of intimacy and communication with the Lord.

If you have never heard God's voice or do not always hear from God, I encourage you to first read the appendix to learn how to consistently hear God's voice.

CHAPTER ONE

Rest, Rest, Rest

One day the Lord spoke to me and He said, "Bill, you need to rest."

I said, "Okay, Lord," and went out to work. My wife has told me that I never rest, that I am always busy. My kids have said the same thing. To me, the idea of lying on the couch or on a beach was not really inviting—it did not bring me joy. I liked being busy and I liked making things, so rest was not something I understood or, quite frankly, wanted to do.

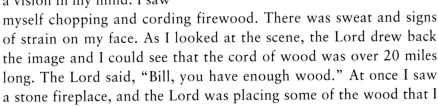

Each time I spoke with the Lord, He said, "Bill, you need to rest."

I said, "Okay, Lord," and went off to work.

One day, He said, "Bill, you need to rest, rest, rest."

I said, "Lord, I don't know what You mean, rest, rest, rest."

Immediately I had a vision in my mind. I saw myself chopping and cording firewood. There was sweat and signs of strain on my face. As I looked at the scene, the Lord drew back the image and I could see that the cord of wood was over 20 miles long. The Lord said, "Bill, you have enough wood." At once I saw a stone fireplace, and the Lord was placing some of the wood that I had cut into the fireplace, and He lit it. I could feel the warmth of the fire.

In front of the fireplace there were two high-backed red leather chairs. The Lord invited me to sit in one of the chairs. He sat in the other chair. As I sat in the chair enjoying the fire and the company of the Lord, I felt a deep sense of rest flow into my soul. I felt at peace, at rest, and I could have sat there all day. I did not feel anxious or feel like I needed to do something. I could see the Lord, but I could not see His face. He said, "Bill, when I say you need to rest, this is what I mean. I want you to come and sit in this chair and spend time with Me. I want to talk with you."

Each day after this experience, I would start my day remembering the vision and sitting back in the red leather chair. Sometimes the Lord was not there but eventually He would come. I would look at Him, and we would discuss the day ahead, and He would counsel me.

One day the Lord did not show up. I looked around the room and realized that the fireplace was in a log cottage. In the room I saw a round dining table with two chairs and a bed by a window. Then I noticed a front door. I walked out the front door onto a covered porch, and the Lord was sitting there in a rocking chair. There was another rocker, and He invited me to sit with Him. For the first time, I could see His face. I could see His eyes, His smile; He had a kind of knowing grin. I was captivated by His face. I wanted to see Him, talk to Him, and look at Him.

While we talked, I realized that the covered porch went around all four sides of the cottage. There was a railing on the porch. The cottage was on a lake, and a blue dock extended out into the lake. On the right side of the cottage, there was a two-storey building with a large double door on the front. On the left side of the cottage was a large horse field, which was enclosed with a white picket fence about five feet high. A road ran along the fence, and farther down the road, I could see a small white barn. Directly in front of the cottage, there was a tree that had all the branches cut off and it looked rather dead. Across the lake I could see a hill covered with trees.

The Lord said, "Do you want to race?"

I said, "Sure." The Lord took off and started to run towards the water, and I chased after Him. He ran onto the dock and then out on the water. I ran after Him on the water. When it became obvious that I would not be able to catch Him, I tackled Him and we went head over heels across the top of the water. We laughed together, and the humour of the situation transformed my heart.

I have visited this place a thousand times since the Lord first introduced me to it. I start my day by saying, "Lord, where would You like to meet me?" and in few moments I can see Him in this special place. It is our secret place, a place where we meet, we talk, and I have learned to rest.

Several months after this experience, I was driving home from work and started feeling a lot of chest pain. I had been experiencing some chest pain for a while and was taking an antacid because I thought it was just gas, but the pain did not go away. At the time I was managing a large network rebuild project for a local steel mill and the project was having a lot of trouble. The pain became severe. I called my doctor, and he told me to go to the hospital.

I was immediately admitted to the hospital and put on an ECG machine. I was having severe angina. I was given some drugs and transferred to a private room. I was put on oxygen and nitro-glycer-ine, but the pain did not leave me. I knew I was in trouble.

As I laid in my bed, I became aware of an angel in my room. My eyes were closed, but I could see him in my mind. When I opened my eyes and looked around the room, I could still see the image of the angel in my mind. I saw the room with my eyes and the angel with the eyes of my heart. Both images were overlaid in my mind, and I could see where the angel was standing and what he looked like. He was a warrior angel dressed in full battle dress. He wore a sword, chain mail, and a helmet. The Lord said, "Bill, you have been promoted. You have a warrior angel assigned to you." That Sunday evening I prayed and asked God to heal me.

On Monday morning, I went for an angiogram. The angel went with me into the operating room. However, in my mind's eye, I was sitting in the red leather chair. The doctor performed the angiogram, and to his amazement there was no blockage and my blood pressure and cholesterol level had dropped. He told me that there was nothing wrong with me except that my arteries were not connected to my heart in the normal way. At some point during this experience, the pain left me and I have not had angina since.

Later I asked the Lord about this event, and this is what He said to me:

Son,

You were not giving Me the burdens of your job. You continued to focus on your own ability. I am your strength, I am your provider, you are not a beast of burden, and My yoke is easy. When you take on a yoke that is not the right one, your soul strains, worry comes, stress manifests, and your body starts to fail. This is what happened at the steel mill. Always bring your work and your workload to Me, and I will give you the right yoke that you are to carry, not the one you think you should carry.

Son,

For your whole life you have struggled to provide for your family and have tried to figure out how to raise your salary. You are a competent worker, and I bless that diligence, but you take on too much responsibility. You take on things that are not your responsibility; this is what we must always talk about. You are responsible to walk honestly with man and walk in dependency with Me.

Love, Dad

God is a healing God. He heals both our physical and spiritual hearts. The physical healing of my heart happened rather quickly; however, the spiritual healing of my heart would take much longer. As I have spent time with the Lord, He has healed my spiritual heart as well.

Personal Action

The Lord tells us about a secret place where we can dwell with Him.[3] I encourage you to ask the Lord where He would like to meet with you, where His secret place for you is. As described in the Appendix, I have found that it is always best to focus the eyes of your heart on the Lord before you start writing down your thoughts. To do this, I recommend simply imagining a Bible story that Jesus is in. When you can see the scene and see Jesus, your heart is focused on the Lord. When you can see Him and your heart is fixed on Him, ask Him this question:

1. Lord, where would You like to meet with me?

2. Write down what the Lord says or shows you.

3. Call a friend and read to them what the Lord gave to you.

4. Ask them if their heart bears witness that it came from the Lord.

CHAPTER TWO

The Cottage

My secret place has many parts. The location the Lord chooses to meet me usually contributes to the lesson and reinforces the message.

One day I was waiting in the leather chair by the fireplace, but the Lord did not come. I called the Lord, and still He did not come. I got out of the chair and walked out the front door, and I saw the Lord standing at the end of the porch on the left side of the cottage. I went to Him and asked Him, "Why didn't You answer me when I called?"

He replied, "I love it when you come looking for Me." He had a wonderful smile of delight.

Another time I was upset about some things that were happening at work. It appeared that other people were being preferred or promoted over me. I felt it was unjust. I was older and had more experience, more education, and I had served longer. I was upset, so I went to the Lord. I looked for Him, and again He was not in the red chair. I looked around the room and saw Him sitting at the round dining table. There was a chess board in front of Him. He said nothing; He simply studied the chessboard. Eventually He moved a piece, and then He looked at me and said, "Son, I move the pieces on the chessboard."

Immediately in my spirit I was convicted. I had been thinking man was in charge, but God reminded me that He is the one in charge. The Lord showed me by this illustration that He is in charge of my activities and man is not. I repented of not trusting Him and forgave those whom I felt had overlooked me. I acknowledged my Father was in charge. That day I learned that He closes doors that should not be opened and opens doors no man can close.

The Jam Shack

One weekend my wife, Sue, and I were ministering in another city. When we came home, I went to the Lord and I saw Him in an orchard. The orchard was behind the cottage and had two rows of fruit trees. The trees were covered with fruit. Some of the branches were so heavy, they required supports to hold them up. There were bushel baskets on the ground. I saw the Lord picking fruit and putting it in the baskets.

The fruit was similar in colour to an apple, but it was much larger, more like the size of a Korean pear. He picked up a bushel of the fruit, and we walked toward a small building located at the end of the orchard. It was a very pretty building. It was quite different from the cottage. The cottage is a log building, whereas this building reminded me of a Swiss chalet. It was painted white with decorative carved white scalloped edging all along the roof line. The covered front porch had a railing with spindles that were also painted white.

We went into the building, and there was large table in the

middle of the room and rows of shelves along the walls. On each shelf there were small Mason jars of preserves. Each one of the jars was carefully labelled. The Lord took some of the fruit from the basket and did some type of processing and filled a new jar with the result. He then carefully labelled the jar and placed it on the shelf. He said, "Son, that is the fruit you produced this weekend." As I looked at the jars, I could see the names of all the places we had ministered. I realized that the Lord records everything we do for Him and lovingly labels a jar with the results.

It takes time to produce fruit. Our Father is the gardener, and He will cultivate us so that we bring forth the greatest fruit. However, we have a responsibility in the process as well. Here is something the Lord spoke to me about this.

Son,

I have encouraged you to write this book. You need to write the book; however, it takes effort to write and publish. It takes work. We are designed to work together. A yoke has two places, a spot for Me and a spot for you. Together we will move the load to completion. My portion of the load is different than yours. You are designed to carry a specific load.

Son,

You still need to carry your part of the load for the work to be completed. I will inspire you to write, I will provide wisdom and people to help you publish the book. I will grant you favour with editors. I will give you people to buy the book, but you must write it. This is how the kingdom of God works. Together we build. You have a part to do, and so do I; however, if you do not do your part, it won't happen.

Love, Dad

The Lord encourages us to take steps of faith; however, that does not mean we have to perform for Him to receive His love. God loves us just the way we are. If we never do another thing for God, He would not love us any less, and if we became the next Billy Graham, He would not love us any more. God loves us because we are His children, not for the things we do for Him. His love does not depend on us loving Him either. The Bible declares that *"God demonstrates His own love for us in this: While we were still sinners Christ died for us."*[4] This simply means that before we had ever done anything for Him or even anything good He loved us. God is Love.

However, God remembers everything we do for Him. He cherishes our acts of kindness and the simple acts of service we perform. He calls these acts the fruit of our life. The Lord demonstrated this truth to me in the jam shack, and my hope is that you too will see that He remembers every good thing that you do and will reward you for it.

Personal Action

When Jesus was asked what was the greatest commandment, He replied, *"Love the Lord your God with all your heart and with all your soul and with all your mind and with all your strength."*[5] Our strength includes our abilities. This whole exhortation has to do with loving God with our skills and talents. Perhaps you have felt the Lord has encouraged you to use your abilities to love Him, but you are not sure how to do it. He wants to help you to develop fruit in your life, and He wants to help you with the calling and purpose He has written on your heart.

1. List the things that you have wanted to do or have felt the Lord encourage you to do.

2. Ask the Lord what He has to say about these things and how could you start to move forward with Him to accomplish some of them.

3. Write down what the Lord says or shows you.

4. Call a friend and read to them what the Lord gave to you.

5. Ask them if their heart bears witness that it came from the Lord.

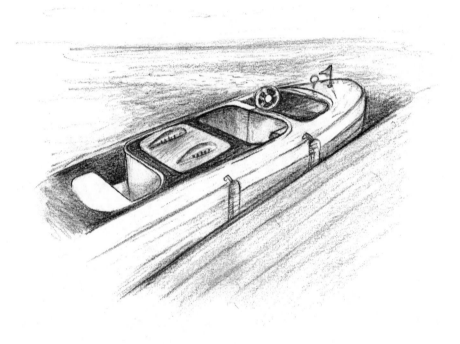

CHAPTER THREE

The Boathouse

There is a boathouse located on the right side of the cottage. It is a two-story board-on-board building with a peaked roof and large double doors on the front and back. There is also a small window on the second floor. Inside the boathouse, there is a workshop with a long carpenter's bench along the left wall. There is a window over the carpenter's bench. In the corner there is a pot-bellied stove and two stumps to sit on. I have been to the workshop many times.

The first time I visited the workshop, there was a partially built boat lying upside down on two sawhorses. I did not pay much attention to it; I just sat with the Lord in front of the pot-bellied stove and we talked. Another time I came to the workshop and I saw the Lord working on something and I asked Him, "What are you making?"

He opened His hand, and I saw a fully grown miniature tree. He said, "I am making a tree. If I can make a tree, is there anything too hard for Me?"

On the right side of the workshop, there is another long workbench and stairs that lead to the second floor. On the second floor, there is a writing table and chair under the window. The Lord and I have met upstairs a few times. The last time we met there, the Lord placed paper on the writing desk and told me to write this book.

One day the Lord said, "Son, come with Me; I have something to show you." I followed Him along the right side of the boathouse and around to the water's edge. Here there was a boat slip, and in the slip was a brand new cedar-strip inboard speedboat, the kind you would see at an historic Muskoka cottage. I have always admired the older inboard speedboats with their fine brass fittings. The Lord said, "Son, I made this for you." I was overwhelmed. I could not believe He would do this for me. I had never mentioned to anyone that if I could ever have a boat, it would look just like this. Even though the speedboat was an unspoken desire of my heart, the Lord provided it for me.

When the Lord asked if I would like to go for a ride, I of course said yes. He backed the boat out of the slip. I could hear the deep throated thunder of the inboard engine spring to life, and we were away, clipping over the waves. I loved it. I could see the Lord's hair blowing back and the smile on His face, and then suddenly we lifted off the water and we were flying. I could see the entire area, the cottage, the orchard, the boathouse, and the lake we were on. I asked the Lord, "Is this the mansion You have prepared for me?" I knew that the Bible said that Jesus was going to prepare a place for us, so I wondered if this was it.

The Lord said, "No, Son, this is not Heaven, it is just a place we can meet where you are comfortable. Heaven is much more wonderful."

Once while I was on a holiday, the Lord asked me, "Bill, what are your goals?"

My initial reaction was, "God, why are You asking me this? I am on my holidays; goals are for work." However, after some discussion, I took out a piece of paper and started to write out my life goals. I wrote down things I would like to own, what I wanted to do, what I wanted for my children, what my ministry dreams were. When I finished, I realized that I had written out my heart's desires and immediately I knew why the Lord had asked me to do this. He had me write them down so that as He began to give them to me, I would know that I had desired them.

I had written down about twelve goals, and while many of them have come to pass, some still have not. Some had to do with ministry, and some did not. One of my goals was to minister all over the world. Since then we have ministered on five continents.

I also told the Lord that I wanted to play the violin. I did not have a violin, nor could I afford one, but God is big. When I got home from my holiday, I spoke to a friend about my desire to learn the violin. He happened to have one that he did not need and was willing to sell it. It was not the best quality, but it was also not expensive so I bought it and started to take lessons. A few years later, my aunt died and left me her very expensive violin. I had never mentioned to her that it was my heart's desire to play the violin, yet God knew, and today I play a very fine instrument.

Another one of my heart's desires seemed like a dream. I wanted an MGB sports car. I love old cars. I had taken auto mechanics in school and really enjoyed the older automobiles; but I had children in university and lots of bills, so while this desire was nice, it was hardly realistic.

About a year after I had written the list, I was telling my friend Dave about how the Lord had told me to write down my life goals and I mentioned that I wanted an MGB. He stopped me and said, "Bill, you have to see what I have in my garage at work." Dave installs doors and windows for a living, and as we entered his shop, I saw a pristine, certified, 1974 Porsche 914 sports car. He said, "Bill, I was installing windows on a house and after I was finished, the customer said, 'Dave, I just lost my job. I can't pay for the windows, so take my sports car as payment.' So I did. Bill, you can have this car for the price of the windows on his house. Pay me when you can." We had needed another car, so this was God sent, and although all I wanted was an MGB, my Father in Heaven provided a Porsche.

All of us have hidden desires. These desires may be for things we would like to own or things we would like to do. We may feel awkward discussing these publicly because we are afraid we will appear greedy or selfish. I asked the Lord about the topic of heart's desires and this is what He said.

Son,

All men and women have desires, most of them are good, but some are not. When you consider your desires, you need to test them. If you desire something that is contrary to the law, like inappropriate sexual activity, or if you covet a man's wife, horse, or house, I will not bless this.

First you need to examine your desires. Do not desire something that I have told you in My word you are not to have. If your desires are not contrary to My revealed word, I will give them to you; however, many people desire possessions or position as status symbols to build themselves up and embrace an identity related to the object of their desires. I will not bless this. I will not provide this. I will only provide you a desire of your heart if it will draw you closer to Me. You must first delight in the Lord, and then I will give you the desires of your heart.

Love, Dad

Personal Action

Your Heavenly Father wants to give you the desires of your heart. You may be like me and need to write them down to help you identify them. This way when the Lord starts to give them to you, you will know you wanted them. At Christmas, my wife and I love to give gifts to our children. We ask them what they want and listen carefully, and if at all possible, we give them what they ask. We delight in giving our kids their hearts' desire—so does your Heavenly Father. Don't be afraid to be honest with Him and tell Him what your heart wants. Scripture says that if you delight in Him, He will give you your heart's desire because He loves you.[6]

1. Make a list of your heart's desires and your life goals.

2. Ask the Lord to provide them for you.

3. Ask Him, "Lord, what do You have to say about my heart's desires?"

4. Call a friend and read to them what the Lord gave to you.

5. Ask them if their heart bears witness that it came from the Lord.

CHAPTER FOUR

The Avenue of Life

There is a road that extends away from the cottage to the outskirts of the secret place. To the right, the road passes a small church and two fields. One is for horses and the other is for sheep. There is fence between the two fields. At the far end of the road, there is a small white barn. I have called the road to the left of the cottage the Avenue of Life. On the Avenue of Life, there are additional houses. At the end of the road, there is nothing; the vision stops. I believe this is because my life is not over. The Lord has much more for me to do, and as my life unfolds, I am confident more of the road will appear.

Each house on the Avenue of Life has a name that relates to a part of my life. One of the houses has my company's name on it; another has my church's name on it. Often when the Lord wants to talk to me about an issue at work, we will meet in the house belonging to work. Inside this house, there are different rooms relating to different aspects of my work.

One day at work, I was in a marketing meeting. We were struggling to create a new marketing tag line for a program we were developing. A marketing tag line is a short statement that embodies a value or truth about a product, such as "Things go better with Coke." We were having no success. I decided to inquire of the Lord and ask Him for a marketing tag line. He gave me a tag line, and I read it to the group, and they said, "Bill, that is brilliant. Where did you get that?" I learned that day that God can give you ideas for business, and He is very comfortable working in the business realm.

As a strategist I develop "Thought Leadership Seminars" that convey breakthrough concepts. I use creative techniques and methods to help customers look at their business problems. One day I had done some market research on the needs of customers and found that the top thing customers wanted to know was how to reduce the cost of information technology in their companies.

I continued to research this question. After reading thousands of pages of material, I had many theories and new methods, but I had no idea how to sort out the information or how to communicate it in a clear and concise way. Looking at the foot-high stack of white papers and articles on my desk, I felt that it was impossible to make it simple. I said, "Lord, how do I sort this out? How can I convey this information to another person?" The Lord spoke to me and said,

> Bill,
>   There are three categories of cost that make up an IT budget: technology, people, and facilities.
> * In the technology realm, the goal is to improve asset utilization. Sort out all your ideas for improving asset utilization here.
> * In the people realm, sort out all your ideas for eliminating work or for compressing the time it takes to do a task.
> * In the facilities area, sort out all your ideas for improving electrical and space efficiency.

He spoke so simply, yet it was so profound.

This revelation became the foundation for an IT transformation marketing program and an IT transformation planning workshop. It has helped me leverage millions of dollars in sales for my firm and enabled to me develop IT transformation plans for companies and governments all over the world. It all started by asking God, "How do I solve this problem?"

Problem solving requires both creative thinking and wisdom. "Wisdom is a deep understanding of people, things, events or situations, resulting in the ability to choose or act to consistently produce the optimum results with a minimum of time and energy."[7] The Bible says, *"If any of you lacks wisdom, he should ask God, who gives generously to all without finding fault, and it will be given to him."*[8]

God's wisdom is not limited to spiritual things; it also includes earthly things like cost-reduction strategies and technical insight. This was another significant revelation for me. I never thought that God could, or would even want to, give me specific technical intuition for seminars and programs. It was only when I was in a time of crisis that I called on Him for help with a technical problem, and when I did, He answered me.

Wonderful Wisdom

On one occasion I was struggling with two quite unrelated issues. The first was a business problem for a company that had been very difficult to work with. The second was more personal as I was disturbed with the killing of Christians in India. At the time, I was going to India to teach a leaders' school, so the situation in India was quite frightening. Both of these issues were laying heavily on my heart. As I drove along the highway, I discussed them with the Lord.

I saw Him invite me into a speedboat on the lake in the secret place, and we went for a ride. As we drove along, I saw a man on the shore waving at us. The Lord drove the boat to the shore, and I asked, "Lord, who is the man?"

He replied, "It is Peter; he has something he wants to teach you."

I got out of the boat. Peter was dressed in a white robe and had a beard and long hair. He said, "Bill, I want to show you a better way to fish." He then tied a hook on a line in a way that the hook could freely float on the line. He said, "This lets the hook move easily on the line so the worm moves and is more attractive to the fish. If you are more flexible with the company you are dealing with, you will catch more fish." Peter's words directly addressed my problem with the difficult company.

I got back into the boat, and the Lord drove further down the lake. Another man was waving from the beach, and the Lord drove the boat to the shore. Again I asked, "Who is this?"

The Lord said, "It is Ezekiel; he has something he wants to tell you."

Ezekiel said, "Bill, the angels who are with you are much larger than the enemy who is coming against you." This was a direct word of encouragement to not fear going to India.

I got back into the boat, and the Lord drove further down the lake where another man was on the shore. The Lord drove the boat to the shore. I asked "Who is this?"

The Lord said, "It is John, my beloved."

John spoke to me and he said, "They tried to kill me, and even though they tried, they could not. Trust in the Lord to protect you." The vision ended.

John's words were very specific and encouraging. As a result, I felt a level of boldness rise up in me.

Initially I was concerned about this vision because I was talking to saints. Warning bells started to go off in my head, so I discussed it with a friend to whom I am accountable. He reminded me that Jesus did the very same thing. He said, "Bill, I don't have any theological concerns with this because Jesus did exactly the same thing on the Mount of Transfiguration, and if He can do it, so can you. The Bible tells us that those who went before us are not dead. They are alive in the presence of the Lord, and New Jerusalem contains the spirits of righteous men made perfect."[9]

I believe experiences have to be measured by scripture and the fruit. This was the only time I have ever spoken with the saints. I was not seeking counsel from saints, they just appeared in the vision and it was the Lord Jesus who introduced them to me. It was unusual, but it produced faith and gave me great counsel.

After this experience, Sue and I went to Mumbai. We landed on the day the terrorists were killing people in the streets. We were locked down in our hotel, and I was glad the Lord had prepared us with the vision ahead of time. Scripture says that *"The angel of the Lord encamps around those who fear Him and he delivers them."*[10] We knew this was true in Mumbai, and we were at peace.

Personal Action

There are many facets to our lives, and the Lord is interested in every one of them. He is not limited to only the "church" part of your life. He wants to give us counsel and wisdom for every decision we make, whether it is work, family, or church related. However we do need to ask Him. We need to involve Him in our decisions.

1. In what areas of your life do you need wisdom?

2. List specific problems for which you need wisdom.

3. Ask the Lord for His wisdom, advice, and counsel for each problem.

4. Write down what He says.

5. Call a friend and read to them what the Lord gave to you.

6. Ask them if their heart bears witness that it came from the Lord.

CHAPTER FIVE

The Barn

In the secret place, there is a small white barn at the end of the road. The first time I visited the barn, I saw the Lord shoeing a horse. In this vision, He was carefully nailing on the horseshoes. I was surprised to see Him doing this manual task. I have met the Lord many times in the barn, and each time we have met, we have talked about caring for sheep. The barn is one of my favourite places. It is there I feel His heart for the Body of Christ.

There was a time when I was asked to co-pastor a new church. I was not certain if this was good idea, and I asked the Lord what He thought. He gave me a dream. In the dream, I saw the sheep pen beside the barn. Initially there were only a few sheep in the pen, but soon the sheep pen was full. There was a fence between the sheep pen and the horse field, so I opened the gate and let the sheep flood out onto the horse field. I loved being with the sheep. I realized that the sheep were unable to speak when they had a problem. If they got thorns in their feet or faces, they could not help themselves. However, I could see the anguish in their hearts by looking in their eyes.

Psalm 23 states, *"The Lord is my shepherd...He anoints my head with oil."* This psalm describes the role of the shepherd and his responsibility to care for his sheep. To help his sheep, a shepherd must be involved in their lives; to find and pull out thorns, to anoint their wounds with oil so they can heal. As I looked out over the field, I saw thousands of sheep. I said, "Lord, I cannot take care of all of these sheep."

He said, "Son, I will send helpers to work with you." Immediately I saw people throughout the field caring for and feeding the sheep. The dream of the sheep and the vision of Jesus taking care of the horse encouraged me to step out and start helping this church.

I soon realized that although I had a deep heart for God's church and particularly His sheep, pastoring in this particular church was not the way God had planned for me to accomplish this area of calling in my life. We blessed the other pastor to care for the church and stepped down. This experience left me deeply puzzled. I asked the Lord, "Why did You encourage me to do this? Why did You give me such a deep heart for this ministry and for the sheep?"

The Lord reminded me of another dream He had given me before this church was started. In this dream, I saw a map of a land I had never seen. I saw towns with names I did not know. I was on one side of a mountain range, and the towns were on the other side near a lake. I saw myself and my wife getting into a car with another man and his wife. We were all very excited about the trip. The car was a brand new 1920s Ford Model T. We were all wearing fur coats because we had to go over the mountain and it was going to be cold. I was also driving from the back seat. When I asked the Lord what the dream meant, He said,

Son,

You have in your heart to go to a land you have not been to before, to places you have not seen. The journey will require you to cross a high mountain. You are going with another couple, and although you could get there in a Ford Model T, it would be much better to go in a new car that is faster and has heat; also, you cannot drive from the back seat. Son, I gave you this dream so you would know when you have to step down because you will not be allowed to use the new methods you want to. I foretold this to you so when it happens, you will know that it is all in My hands.

You also needed to pastor this work so you could see that your vision is not for a local church alone but for the body of Christ as a whole. You also needed to be asked to pastor this church in your area because if your pastor had overlooked you, it would have hurt you for the rest of your life. This was a kindness.

Love, Dad

The lesson was a hard lesson. I was broken-hearted that it did not go the way I had hoped. As my wife and I recalled the dream, we realized how symbolic it had been of our situation during that time in our lives. We also recognized that it was no surprise to God; He knows the beginning and the end of all. The Lord pastored me through this difficult time.

Personal Action

The Lord may have taken you through a similar situation. We need to be honest with God when we feel let down by Him or others. We need to share with Him how we really feel and express our fears, our frustrations, and our hopes, face to face. He is able to listen to us as we really are. We do not need to put on an air of righteousness and deny how we really feel. He is bigger than how we feel.

Have you ever been asked to do something that has not worked out? Perhaps like me, you felt led to do it, but eventually you stepped down or, worse, were asked to leave. God knows that this has caused you great pain and caused you to question Him. He wants to answer those questions.

1. Write out a short letter to the Lord telling Him how you feel, and write down the questions you have about the situation.

2. Ask the Lord, "Why did this happen?"

3. Ask the Lord to answer your questions.

4. Call a friend and read to them what the Lord gave to you.

5. Ask them if their heart bears witness that it came from the Lord.

CHAPTER SIX

The Church

In the secret place there is a very small church that is no more than eight feet wide and eight feet long. It only has two rows of pews. Outside the church is a garden that is about eight by twelve feet. Previously I had seen the Lord cultivate the soil and plant seeds in this garden, and over a short period of time I watched the crops grow. As the crops grew, He continued to care for the garden. There was corn at the back of the garden and shorter crops in the front. Jesus is our shepherd, but our Father is a gardener. I did not understand what the garden meant, so I asked the Lord. He said,

Son,
The garden is a representation of your ministry. It is outside the church. It will grow and flourish, but it is not inside the church. There will be many different types of crops. They are not all the same. The crops represent my people. They are all destined to different roles in My kingdom. You will care and teach and minister to My body. Son, the church is important, but it is a very small part of your ministry; your ministry is outside the church.

Over the next year, I started to see more garden plots being prepared. Each one was the same size, and they appeared all along the fence on both sides of the church. First the ground was marked to indicate where the garden was to be cut, and then the plots were prepared for planting. We as the body of Christ are called to change the world.

We cannot do this inside the four walls of a church building. We too need to cultivate the Lord's gardens outside the churches in our communities and bring His kingdom to His world.

Recently the Lord has been telling believers all over the world that it is time to get out of the church and go out into the world and make a difference. The Lord wants us to see that we all have a specific calling and purpose in His world. Loren Cunningham describes society's spheres of influence as seven mountains. He lists the seven mountains[11] as:

1. Religion
2. Family
3. Education
4. Government
5. Media and Communication
6. Arts and Entertainment
7. Business

We are all called to influence the world in at least one of these spheres. For most of us, these mountains are the places we work or spend most of our time. We are called by the Lord to bring His wisdom into these realms, and by doing so, men will see our good work and want to know this God who gives us such wisdom.

The church is also changing. Today more and more Christians are leaving conventional church models. They still love the Lord and want to know Him. They love to worship and fellowship; they just don't want to go to a conventional church. As a result, less formal church models such as house groups and informal groups of believers are starting to spring up. These informal groups meet, share and love one another, and are committed to bringing the kingdom to their community. This is not actually a new church model, but is in fact a very old church model. It is a New Testament church model.

I love the Lord's church, and I love His body, and I know that there are many wonderful churches and alternative church models. I feel that the Lord is seeking out His entire church, many members of which are outside the four walls of a conventional church. For example, in China there are few big church buildings and the church is quite fluid in its structure, yet it is growing at an unprecedented rate. In Canada we are also seeing a growth in home churches as well. We have had the privilege of meeting and teaching in these home churches and have found that these intimate and personal sessions produce deep relationships within the body of believers and with the Lord.

Personal Action

Many people have preconceived opinions regarding how church should be structured and conducted. The challenge for us as believers is not to limit our definition of church to a building, a denomination, or our previous worship experience. Unfortunately this is easier said than done. We become comfortable with formality and structure and can start thinking that our definition of worship, our church experience, is the best way, the right way, the only way. God is not quite so limiting. He is new every morning and is very capable of adapting to different groups of people.

1. Ask yourself, do you accept that alternative worship models such as a home church, internet church, or an informal gathering of believers, are a viable alternative to conventional Sunday morning church services?

   Yes ❑   No ❑

2. Do you have vision for new ways of being an expression of the Lord's church?

3. Ask the Lord what His vision is for His church in this age.

4. We all have a unique role to play in God's kingdom. Ask the Lord how you can bring His kingdom to the realm to which you have been called.

5. Call a friend and read to them what the Lord gave to you.

6. Ask them if their heart bears witness that it came from the Lord.

CHAPTER SEVEN

The Motorcycle

I have worried for most of my adult life. I don't remember it being a problem when I was a teenager, but as I got older, the more I struggled with worry and anxiety. I would memorize verses in the Bible like *"Do not be anxious about anything, but in everything, by prayer and petition, with thanksgiving, present your requests to God,"*[12] but I would still worry. No matter how many Bible verses I memorized, I would still worry, I would still be afraid; faith just seemed to elude me. I knew God's word, but I did not have faith in Him.

When I started hearing from God and writing down what He said, I noticed that Jesus seemed to have all the time in the world for me. He was never in a hurry. I could ask Him any question I wanted, and He would answer me. This was an amazing breakthrough in my relationship with God. I had always loved His written word, and at times it had given me great comfort. Yet when He spoke to me, it was different. When He spoke to me I felt acceptance, love, hope, and joy. I felt faith. A verse in the bible states *"Faith comes from hearing the message, and the message is heard through the word of Christ."*[13] When Jesus spoke to me, I found faith rise up in my heart much more consistently than when I just read the verse. God's spoken word produced faith.

I do not particularly like travelling, and although I have been to twenty-seven countries, I still find that travel can make me feel uptight. One of the first overseas trips Sue and I planned was to Mozambique. I was anxious, so I went to the Lord and told Him how I felt. I saw the Lord on a big chrome motorcycle out in front of the cottage. He was putting a bed roll on the back of the bike, and He was happy. I could see excitement and joy on His face. There were three seats on the bike. In the next scene, Susan and I were sitting behind Jesus on the bike as He was driving down the road. His hair was blowing back, and I noticed that He was not wearing a helmet. All of a sudden it struck me: *Of course He does not need to wear a helmet, He can't have an accident, He is in control of everything.* I then challenged myself, *Why am I worrying about this trip? When Jesus is in the driver's seat nothing can happen to us. He is in control.*

Another time, I was specifically bothered by a trip to Iceland. It was a complex trip that required changes in London and Oslo and an overnight stay in London. My experience at Heathrow in the past had not been positive, so I was not looking forward to the trip. Many of my fears were ridiculous, but still I was hounded by thoughts like we would not get the seats we asked for, the luggage would get lost, we would oversleep and miss the plane, we would not be able to find a cab in London, and so on. I asked the Lord, "What should I do about this? How should I pray?" He spoke to me and said,

Son,
    Declare what I am going to do for you. Be specific; here, let Me show you.
    1. You (the Lord) will ensure we get the seats on the plane.
    2. You will ensure we get there on time.
    3. You will protect our luggage from getting lost.
    4. You will provide a cab to the hotel.
    5. You will ensure we don't oversleep.
    6. You will ensure we can get a cab to the airport in the morning.
    7. You will ensure we will not miss our plane to Oslo.
    8. You will ensure we will not miss our connection to Iceland.
    9. You will provide us with a place to stay in Iceland.
    10. You will provide someone to look after us.

I declared the statements just as the Lord had told me to and everything went well, and even though the plane to Oslo was late, we still made our connection. The Lord taught me to take the offensive, to take captive the thoughts that were not from Him and to declare what He was going to do. This was a great lesson for me. Scripture states,

"We demolish arguments and every pretension that sets itself up against the knowledge of God, and we take captive every thought to make it obedient to Christ."[14] Through this experience, the Lord taught me how to apply this Bible verse to my life.

After I had done the declaration, I asked the Lord, "Isn't it rather presumptuous of me to declare that You will do something without asking You?" He said,

> Son,
> You can always declare I will do what is in My character and in My written word. I heal, I protect, I am your strong tower. I am your shield and strength. I will never leave you, I will never never forsake you. You can always declare I will do these things because I said I would.

I began to realize that worry and anxiety were actually idolatry. When I worried, I was actually saying God was smaller than what I worried about. When I worried, I was choosing to bow down and worship the thing I was worrying about. I had made it an idol. I repented of idol worship and declared, "God, You are bigger than what I worry about."

Personal Action

We are encouraged by the Lord to *"present your requests to God. And the peace of God, which transcends all understanding, will guard your hearts and your minds in Christ Jesus."*[15] If you lack peace, it is likely an indicator that you have some worry or anxiety in your life. God's will is that we would have peace in our hearts, that we should not have any anxiety.

If you struggle with worry and anxiety, God wants you to have freedom from it. He wants you to have peace in the middle of the storm. If you want to get rid of your worries and fears, please do the following exercise.

1. List what you worry about.   Is God bigger?

                                                  Yes   No
a. _____   ❏   ❏

b. _____   ❏   ❏

c. _____   ❏   ❏

d. _____   ❏   ❏

e. _____   ❏   ❏

f. _____   ❏   ❏

g. _____   ❏   ❏

h. _____   ❏   ❏

i. _____   ❏   ❏

j. _____   ❏   ❏

2. Look at your list and decide if God is bigger than what you are worrying about?

3. Repent of your worries and declare them as idolatry.

4. Write down what God is going to do for you regarding each worry you have listed.

a. You will _____

b. You will _____

c. You will _____

d. You will _____

e. You will _____

f. You will _____

g. You will _____

h. You will _____

i. You will _____

j. You will _____

5. Declare out loud what God is going to do for you.

6. Ask the Lord what He would like to say to you about worry and anxiety in your life and write it down.

7. Call a friend and read to them what the Lord gave to you.

8. Ask them if their heart bears witness that it came from the Lord.

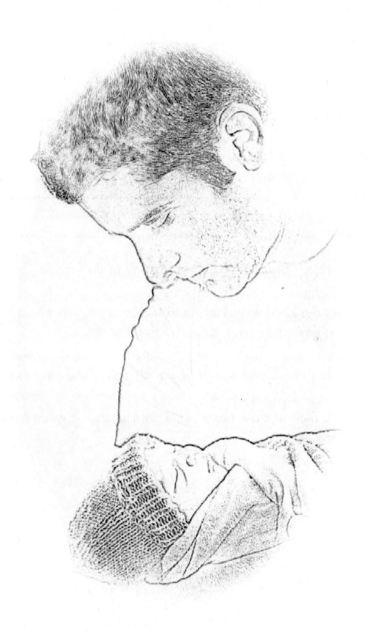

CHAPTER EIGHT

Abba Father

I have always enjoyed listening to God and studying His word, but my relationship with Him has changed as a result of the secret place experience. I am now seeing Him face to face and talking with Him as one man speaks to another. In the past when I prayed, I would often speak quickly the things I would like the Lord to do and I would use scriptures to back up my requests.

I realized I would never speak to another person that way. I would wait until we were settled and then open the conversation with a question about how the person was. I would listen to their response and then begin to discuss whatever I had come to talk with them about. I would not rush or have a one-sided conversation. I am now talking with my Heavenly Father this way. I am quite simply having a conversation. I discuss and reason with Him. Prayer is not a duty, not a formality, but a personal, intimate, truthful, and transparent conversation.

When I read the Psalms, I notice that King David seems to talk to God very transparently. David tells Him exactly how he feels. Now that I am having this type of relationship with my Heavenly Father, I can see that the Psalms are just a record of their conversations.

Jesus came so that we could have this type of relationship with our Heavenly Father. He said, *"I am the way, the truth and the life. No one comes to the Father except through me."*[16] Jesus' goal was that we would come to the Father and have a relationship with Him, just like He did. Jesus' purpose on earth was to break down the wall between us and our Heavenly Father so that we too could call him Abba Father. *Abba* is the Aramaic word for Daddy. Jesus called His Father Abba.[17]

As the Lord took me deeper into the secret place, I stopped calling Him Lord or Father and now I simply call Him Dad. I had never felt comfortable calling God Daddy. I had heard others call Him that but I could not, yet now it seems so natural. I want to call Him Dad. I want to hear what He has to say. I want Him to teach me His word.

Jesus told us that the Holy Spirit would teach us all things. *"But the Counselor, the Holy Spirit, whom the Father will send in my name, will teach you all things and will remind you of everything I have said to you."*[18]

Each day when I meet with the Lord, I start by waiting and asking the Father where He would like to meet. I simply say, "Dad, where would You like to meet today?" Then I wait until the Lord appears in my mind. I wait until I see Him clearly, and I look Him in the face. Often I hug Him and feel His presence. His hugs and looks speak into me more than words. I drink in His acceptance and His love like a sponge, and my worries or problems seem to melt in His presence. He is always smiling. His eyes radiate love and acceptance. His mouth has a perpetual grin like a loving Dad who is just enthralled with His children. I know I always have His full attention and that He is never in a hurry.

My experience has been that the Lord loves relationship. He is far more interested in listening to me and healing my heart than in me storming the gates of some city or situation in spiritual warfare. He is far bigger than any demonic power or stronghold, and He holds the key to unlock strongholds and issues. If I simply spend time with Him and ask Him for wisdom, He will give it to me. Let me cite an example.

One day I was at work and I was feeling discouraged. I felt that I had not accomplished much in my life. I said, "Lord, I am only a project manager."

He said, "Son, you are not a project manager. You are a son of God who does project management." These simple words broke the power of title and position as a measure of my identity and freed me to walk in the truth. I am a son of God. This is my true identity. I am not the title on my business card.

Over the next few years, this revelation became a great help to me because there was considerable turmoil in my industry. My job changed many times, and in man's eyes, it looked as if the new jobs were downgrades from the previous ones. Through all this, the Lord's words kept me strong: "You are a son of God; you are not what your business card says." As a result, the titles and positions held no power over me. If I had been living the lie that I am my job title, I might have been reluctant to take those jobs. Those changes were all ordained by God, and the experience I gained in those positions equipped me to do the job I now have.

There was another time at work when people started to talk about me behind my back. This was not the first time this had happened. I had noticed a cycle in my life, I was either the "golden boy" or "the dog." My managers could never figure out why this happened. Each year I would accomplish many breakthroughs, and then some incident would occur that would undermine me. I went to the Lord and said, "Dad, why am the golden boy and then the dog? Why does this happen?" He said,

Son, bind the lying spirit and loosen blessing over yourself.

I understood the concept of binding the lying spirit, but I had no grid for the concept of loosening blessing. I knew the Bible said *"Whatever you bind on earth will be bound in heaven and whatever you loose on earth shall be loosed in heaven."*[19] However this second part, "loosed on earth and in heaven" was new to me.

Although I did not really understand what the Lord had said, in obedience I declared it, saying, "I bind every lying and deceiving spirit that comes against me and I loosen blessing over myself." To my amazement, immediately all the talking behind my back stopped and my career began to take off. I was promoted, I developed new programs and methods, was promoted again, and the blessing has not stopped. Now whenever I feel some kind of lie forming against me, I pray the same prayer. When I enter a new business situation, I declare, "I loosen blessing over myself."

In the Bible, Nehemiah was not afraid to ask God for favour. When he planned to enter the king's presence he said, *"Give your servant success today by granting him favor in the presence of this man."*[20] Like me, Nehemiah was a program manager who oversaw several large projects, and the Lord loosened blessing over everything to which Nehemiah put his hand. You too can do this. You too can ask God to loosen His blessing over you.

Personal Action

1. Have you ever experienced a sense of worthlessness, a sense that you have not accomplished very much? You may be suffering under the same lie that I was: the lie of false identity. If you have, pray this prayer:

"Dad, I break agreement with the lie that I am what I have accomplished, or what the title on my business card says. I embrace the truth: I am a son (or daughter) of God, and I bind every lying spirit that comes against me, and I loosen blessing over myself."

2. Ask the Lord, "Where would You like to meet today?"

3. Ask the Lord, "What would You like to say to me about being a son (or daughter) of God?"

4. Write down what the Lord says or shows you.

5. If you have had a problem with relationships, ask the Lord, "What would You like to say to me about this?"

6. Write down what the Lord says or shows you.

7. Call a friend and read to them what the Lord gave to you.

8. Ask them if their heart bears witness that it came from the Lord.

CHAPTER NINE

Healing the Heart

The human body is a complex system. All the parts of our physical being must work in unity for our body to function. If one part becomes ill, the rest of the body suffers. In addition to our physical body, we also have our spiritual being. It includes our mind, our soul, and our spirit. The Bible refers to this part of us as our inner man, or our heart. Like our physical body, our spiritual being must also work in unity.

Unfortunately, most of us have issues in our heart due to problems and experiences that have occurred throughout our lives. The secret place is the place where God heals our hearts as we become transparent with Him about our true feelings and invite Him into our pain. He is not limited in His methods or restricted by time. He is God. Here is an example of His remarkable ability to heal our hearts.

Susan and I were celebrating our 30th wedding anniversary, and I wanted to plan a wonderful holiday for us that would be special and a real blessing. We travel extensively together and have been on five continents, and although travelling to foreign countries may sound exciting, it can often be very tiring and unnerving. I really did not want to go to some far-off country. I also fly all the time as part of my job, so I did not want to fly somewhere on my holiday either. For these reasons, we decided to drive to Myrtle Beach in South Carolina. I planned the trip with the Lord and asked Him to be with us and to work out the details. I booked the reservation months in advance. The Lord said, "Son, this will be a wonderful holiday. I have planned a wonderful time for you."

We drove to Myrtle Beach and arrived late Saturday evening. Since it was summer, Myrtle Beach was packed. I went to the front desk of our resort to check in, but they said they had no record of our reservation. Normally I would have become very irate and demanded to see the manager, but for some reason I felt completely undone. I was unable to speak. I had checked with our bank before we left, and I knew that the resort had received our payment. I felt that God had let me down. He had promised me that this was going to be a wonderful holiday and all I could see was that this was going to be a disaster. Where was I going to stay? Where was I going to go? It was 10:00 at night. What was I going to do?

Susan could see that I was undone and simply asked the front desk if they could accommodate us. They said yes, and we paid for another room. When we got to our room, Susan said, "Bill, when I saw you at the front desk you looked like a little boy, not the man I know. Did you feel abandoned?"

Surprisingly I began to cry and said, "Yes. God abandoned me; He is just like my Dad." My father is a very good man. He is faithful to his wife and his children, but his job took him away from home every week until I was seven years old. During that time, I only saw him on weekends and holidays. When I was in my twenties, I asked him why he took a job like that. He told me that the 1950s were a difficult time and he had to take the job; it was all he could get. When I started working and travelling, I realized that it was no fun to be living in hotels and being alone. I started to appreciate what my father had sacrificed for us, as week after week, year after year, he worked in small towns all over Ontario simply to provide for us. However, as a little boy you don't understand this; you just know you don't have your dad at home.

Susan said, "Let's ask God about when this deep sense of abandonment started in your life and what He would like to say to you about it." As we prayed, I remembered a house we had rented on a highway when I was little boy. There had been a terrible storm, and a car door had slammed on my arm and broke it. I saw myself on the couch in our home. I saw neighbours all round me, but no Dad. I was afraid and I wanted my dad, but he was not there. Susan asked, "Where is Jesus in that scene?"

As I looked around the room, I saw Jesus. He came up to me and said, "Son, I have not abandoned you." As He spoke these words, I felt something change in my heart. Susan led me in some prayers, and I forgave my dad for not being there. Immediately I started to experience deliverance and I felt a demonic spirit leave me. The demonic spirit was broken off by the voice of the Lord and my act of forgiveness. Since that day, I have never suffered from a sense of abandonment. It truly was the best holiday I ever had.

Personal Action

1. Have you had a time when you felt abandoned, a time of despair or hopelessness? Describe the circumstances that made you feel that way.

2. Ask God to bring to your memory when this situation began. When you can see it, look for Jesus in the scene. Write down what Jesus says or does.

3. Call a friend and read to them what the Lord gave to you.

4. Ask them if their heart bears witness that it came from the Lord.

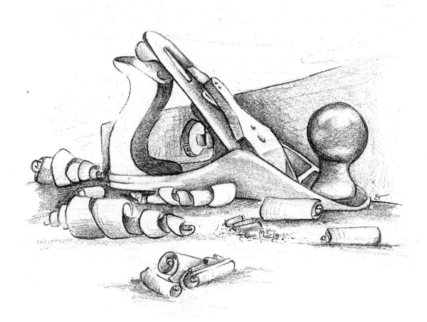

CHAPTER TEN

Hearing God at Work

I work as a strategist for a global computer company. In this role, I provide IT strategies for companies and governments all over the world. A key to my success has been my ability to hear my Heavenly Father's voice. I discuss business problems with Him, and He gives me ideas and wisdom for the company and our customers.

I began to realize that I had a unique intuition for my industry. Several months before my customers would bring an issue to my attention, I would start to feel it in my heart and recognize that it would require an answer. During this preparatory time, I would research the issue and prepare thought leadership seminars on how to solve the problem that was looming on the horizon. I have written many seminars under this sense of intuition, and as a result, I have been able to advise IT managers on new methods to solve problems, advise sales reps on how to create sales, and put consultants to work. This intuition is from God. He gives me the wisdom, the methods, and the insight because He has called me to bring the kingdom of God to the IT world.

As part of my job, I also develop business plans. I was once asked by a firm if I could help them with their business plan. On a flight back from the west coast, I asked the Lord if it would be possible to journal a business plan with Him. A business plan contains six sections. These sections are:

1. Who are your customers?
2. What do they need?
3. What do you sell?

4. How will you deliver your products or services?
5. What are the obstacles to delivering your products and services?
6. How will you be compensated?

As I sat on the plane, I asked the Lord about each section and He began to speak to me. He articulated that the main problem in this particular firm was their method of delivery; He then gave me creative ideas to change their delivery program. When I completed the business plan, I met with the company and I told them what I felt needed to be done in each area. They were amazed. They immediately implemented the program and as a result have seen an expansion of their business.

God is not intimidated by business or business problems. In the Bible, God gave King David specific architectural designs for the temple. He provided the organizational hierarchy for the Levites in the temple. He supplied David with a battle plan to defeat his enemies. Gideon also received specific tactics and a very creative battle plan from the Lord. Using these tactics and methods, Gideon made his army look like a much larger army, and this created great confusion in the enemy's camp, allowing Gideon's army to take the day. The Lord provided these men with specific and practical solutions to real problems. He still does today.

Once I was developing software for a microprocessor system and it would not work. I had no idea what was wrong. I asked my mentor, and he didn't know either. I was stuck. This was a critical problem since it was my job to write this type of software. If I could not solve this problem, I could lose my job. I knelt down and laid hands on my computer and said, "God, I need wisdom to solve this problem by noon." Why I said noon I had no idea. As I continued to work on the problem, I became aware that I had accidently written over the memory. This idea just seemed to pop into my head, and immediately I knew what I had done wrong and was able to solve the problem by noon.

There are many examples of people in the Bible who were not religious leaders yet the Lord said they had unique spiritual talents. Daniel and Joseph were both civil servants and both demonstrated remarkable administrative gifts in governance. The Apostle Paul was an expert in manufacturing and retail sales, making and selling tents everywhere he went. All these men demonstrated excellence in what they did. They were the best in their field, and the world noticed.

The world always notices excellence. I believe this is why Jesus encourages us to *"let your light so shine before men, that they may see your good works, and glorify your Father which is in heaven."*[21] Although this scripture includes acts of philanthropy, the actual Greek word for works is *Ergo,* which includes tasks or employment in its meaning. In the workplace, it is our good work that gets men's attention. When we do good work as a result of receiving God's wisdom, it is God who gets the glory.

I spoke to the Lord about this, and this is what He said.

Son,

Talents often require knowledge to be perfected. Education is critical to developing talents. When you went to Ryerson, you had intuitive knowledge in electronics, yet at Ryerson you filled your knowledge database with the revealed knowledge on the topic.

I can inspire you to do anything, but I work with knowledge. Studying is the process of filling your cognitive ability with data; without it I have no seeds to breathe inspiration on. Read, understand, fill your mind with knowledge, and I will use this as a basis for changing the nation. I want my people to be the best in their field in My kingdom.

Love, Dad

God wants us to be the best we can be. He wants to inspire us, guide us, help us. Trust in Him to be with you as you work.

Personal Action

If you have not asked God for wisdom for your job or whatever you put your hands to every day, I encourage you to ask. Pray with me:

1. I repent for not asking for Your wisdom for my calling, and I ask You to give me wisdom and knowledge to do the work You have given me.

2. List the problems you are facing in your work life and what wisdom you need to overcome them.

3. Ask God for wisdom and answers to these problems, and write down what Jesus says or does.

4. Call a friend and read to them what the Lord gave to you.

5. Ask them if their heart bears witness that it came from the Lord.

CHAPTER ELEVEN

Your Role in the Kingdom

Jesus is very concerned about the kingdom of God and talks about it in the Bible more than 90 times. It is clearly high on His list of priorities. He wants us to understand His kingdom and our responsibilities in that kingdom. He has charged us to make disciples of nations and to teach them what He has commanded us. I have found over 80 things He has commanded us to do, and I feel a deep responsibility to demonstrate those commandments in my workplace.

I know I am called to teach the body of Christ to hear God's voice, to build intimacy with Him, and to encourage the body to seek Him for wisdom in their workplaces and lives. I also know I am called to be a light in the workplace and to bring His kingdom into the business realm.

When I was managing a consulting practice, I was acutely aware of the need to develop good strategies and services so there would be work for the consultants. I felt that God had given me the responsibility to provide them with jobs so they could provide for their families. This sense of responsibly is a God-given part of my calling to break the power of poverty and to create wealth and work for others. It is as much of my calling as preaching and leading worship, and as a result, God gives me the wisdom to do it.

We need to know our calling, our role, and how to shed the shackles of man's expectations and embrace God's destiny for us. We have all been given unique gifts to influence the world for His kingdom. There is no such thing as some jobs being secular and others being sacred. There are just jobs and roles in His kingdom. Some people believe that only ministers are called of God. This is a false belief that limits them from seeing how God has uniquely gifted His people to bring His wisdom and insight to solve the problems of the world. We must discard all false ideas of ministry and embrace our true calling and role in His kingdom.

One situation that illustrates this well occurred at a church. I was speaking about being called to business, and an older man came up to me with tears in his eyes. He said that all of his life he felt he had a calling from God to do his job, but his pastor told him that his job was not a true calling from God, it was just a job. I asked him about what he did. He told me he worked for the Canadian International Development Agency.

The following is the mission and mandate of this agency:[22]

Our Mission

Lead Canada's international effort to help people living in poverty.

Our Mandate

Manage Canada's support and resources effectively and accountably to achieve meaningful, sustainable results and engage in policy development in Canada and internationally, enabling Canada's effort to realize its development objectives.

His job was to give away money on behalf of the Canadian people to help the poor of the world. God had appointed him to do this job. It was a wonderful calling, but he never felt validated by his church. Who better to do this job than a believer who would not be touched by graft and greed?

We all have unique gifts and talents that God has given us for expanding His kingdom here on earth. I discussed this topic with the Lord, and this is what He said.

Son,

I have given you talents and gifts to invest. Investment is not easy work. It takes effort; it takes time to understand how to invest and to understand the nuances of a marketplace. So it is with talents; it takes time to develop them. Practice does make one better; however, do not think you have to be perfect. Start to use your talents, and you will get better.

God wants to provide us with unique intuition to solve real problems in the areas to which we are called to bring His kingdom. I believe God is looking for people to give inventions to in order to solve world problems like the ecology mess, cures for today's economic problems, cures for cancer and other diseases, and even solutions for energy so we can break our dependency on fossil fuels. I believe He wants us to be a part of His kingdom and to bring His ideas for solving these problems. Orville Wright once said, "How is it that the secrets of flight could be hidden for so long?" The answers to all our problems are hidden in God; if we ask Him to unlock those secrets, He will.

Jonas Salk was the doctor who found the cure for polio. I understand that he felt that the polio vaccine wanted to be found and all he had to do was work hard to find it. As I considered this statement, I thought of the millions of prayers from parents asking God to heal their children. I believe God was moved by those prayers and looked for someone to whom He could give the answer. He gave it to Jonas, who was looking for it, and the disease was eliminated. Those parents wanted their children to be healed, but God wanted all children to be healed.

Today the Lord is looking for those who will call on Him for answers to today's problems. He encourages us by saying, *"Ask and it will be given to you; seek and you will find; knock and the door will be opened to you."*[23] Will you be that person?

Personal Action

Many believers do not know what their calling or role is because of the false belief that there are secular and sacred jobs. If you have ever believed that there are secular and sacred jobs, I encourage you to repent of this false belief. Pray with me.

"Father, I repent of the false belief that God doesn't call men and women to so-called secular jobs as their first and primary calling."

To help you sort out your true calling, I have included a simple exercise that will help you honestly face your role in the kingdom of

God. The first step is to list the things that you like to do and what you are good at. Then ask the Lord to help you see the role or calling that would best help you to accomplish this. Remember God wants to give us the desires of our hearts, and that includes what we do for a living.

1. List your talents and strengths.

2. List what you are good at doing, what you are passionate about.

3. List what you feel you have intuition about and a sense of conscience.

4. Look for common activities in the answers to these questions. Your role in the kingdom of God encompasses the activities that are common.

5. Ask the Lord, "What is the best role or calling for me in light of what I like to do and what I am good at?"

6. Write down what He says.

7. Call a friend and read to them what the Lord gave to you.

8. Ask them if their heart bears witness that it came from the Lord.

CHAPTER TWELVE

Living in the Peace of God

The experiences I have described in the previous chapters are as real to me as life itself. I live in both realms. I am seated in this world and in the secret place at the same time. Some ask me how I ensure I am not being misled. I have several safeguards that have helped keep me from getting into trouble.

The Bible states that there is safety in a multitude of counsellors.[24] We are not designed to operate as lone rangers, separated from the body of Christ. In fact, it is quite dangerous to assume that just because we hear from God we don't need to listen to anyone else. This is not the way we are to operate. All words we hear from God are actually prophetic words, and prophetic words must be judged by the body.

To facilitate this in my life, I ask my wife to read my journals. I also ask several men to whom I am accountable to read my journals and give me their honest opinion. Their counsel has been invaluable. If everyone says, "Bill, I don't think that is God," I accept what they say. Occasionally I have had to make a decision where I am not able to get agreement from all those who counsel me. In those situations, I choose to let the peace of God rule in my heart. I felt a couple of examples of this would be appropriate to help you as you walk in your journey of learning to hear the voice of God.

Soon after I became a Christian, my pastor started a program called Training in Ministry. It involved taking Bible school courses by correspondence. I felt the Lord say, "Take the Bible school and be a part of the program." I did not hear God much at that time. In fact, in the 14 years before I learned how to hear from God, I had probably only heard God about five times; however, I was pretty certain God had spoken to me and told me to enrol in this program.

I started the program, and it was very foundational for my Christian walk. I learned both biblical truths and how to preach. However, I struggled with leaving my job and going into "the ministry." Most of my classmates wanted to be pastors, but I was not really sure that I should do that. I love technology. I was given my first electronics set when I was eight years old. I studied electronics in college, and for my entire career I have been involved in the electronics industry.

The trouble was that I was under the false belief that if I really wanted to serve God I had to be in full-time ministry. I had heard of people being called to be a pastor or a missionary, so I thought that those were the only roles available to me. Yet I loved my job; I loved being involved with technology, automating factories, and building test systems. I also loved studying the Bible and preaching. I did not want to miss God's will for my life, but I did not know how to balance these two seemingly opposing interests.

Each summer I struggled with going to Bible school full-time. I had three children and a wife to support, yet in my heart I did not have the peace or perhaps the courage to quit my job and go to Bible school full-time. One summer the Lord spoke to me about this. This was one of the first times I had heard Him. He said,

Son,
    Do you think I am so small that you have to look under rocks to find My will for you? I can make it clear what you are to do.

Love, Dad

This was a revelation for me. I had always felt it would be hard to know what God wanted. Suddenly I knew what to do. I chose to stay working full-time and to study Bible school by correspondence. From this experience, the first truth of hearing the voice of God fell into place:

Truth 1: God wants to talk to me.

A few years later, we had the opportunity to preach at a church because the pastor had left. At the time, this church was in rebellion from my denomination. They had been told not to start the church but said they would do it anyway and, as a result, were asked to leave our denomination. After we preached, they asked us to stay on as pastors. I was reluctant to do this because it meant I would have to leave my denomination. I went to the Lord and said, "This church is in rebellion." I felt the Lord say,

> Son
> The fact they are in rebellion is not your problem. Your problem is will you go?

I felt that the Lord was directly challenging me: whom did I serve, Him or my denomination? This was a very difficult question for me. I loved my denomination—they had taught me and cared for me; however, I said, "I serve You, Lord," so we moved to the community and pastored the church. During this season I never stopped working full-time.

Nearly a year later, Sue and I were asked by the denomination's leadership to attend a meeting where we would receive our license to minister. As we drove to the meeting, I felt that something was wrong, but I didn't know what. I was very agitated and could not figure out why. I thought, *I am about to become a full-fledged minister, so why am I so upset?* Sue and I prayed, and the Lord said, *"Let the peace of Christ rule in your hearts."*[25]

We chose to drive away from the meeting, and immediately we felt peace. It was the first time in months we had felt peace and light; it was as if a great burden had been lifted off us. I had forgotten there could be joy in our lives.

Soon after this, our church elders and I discussed the truth of their rebellion against authority. I asked them what was in their hearts when they started the church. They told me that there was rebellion in their hearts and they repented. Following this, they voted to close the church. I worked with the church elders, the denomination, and the government to close this church, and through it all I learned another truth about hearing God.

Truth 2: God's peace is the referee of what we hear and feel.

If you don't have peace in your heart, it is not likely God you are hearing. Sometimes we do have to make difficult decisions. Sometimes the answers are not that clear. In those times we need to depend on the peace of God and let Him rule.

Personal Action

1. Do you feel there is an issue or situation in your life that robs you of peace? Write out the issue.

2. Focus the eyes of your heart on the Lord and discuss the issue with Him.

3. Write down what Jesus says or does.

4. Call a friend and read to them what the Lord gave to you.

5. Ask them if their heart bears witness that it came from the Lord.

CHAPTER THIRTEEN

Discipline

The examples of hearing from God that I have presented in this book so far have been positive and encouraging. As parents, we have the responsibility to guide and direct our children. Scripture states that *"the Lord disciplines those He loves."*[26] The Lord occasionally disciplines me as well. Let me share some examples of this with you.

One day my son and his friends were playing a computer game in our basement and accidently threw a Wii controller into a fifty-inch TV. The TV screen cracked, and a two-inch spider web fracture formed in the middle of the screen. I was furious. We lived with that broken TV for over a year, and during that time I developed a deep judgment against my son and his friends. I judged them as careless. God tells us *"Do not judge, or you too will be judged. For in the same way you judge others, you will be judged."*[27] I would soon find out first hand what He meant by this scripture.

A year later I bought a new TV to replace the broken one and was mounting it on the wall. I was really afraid that my son and his friends would throw the Wii controller into the new TV, so I was planning to mount a protective screen in front of it. In the process, I dropped a ceiling tile bracket on the TV and scratched the new screen. I was careless and had not covered the screen. The very thing I had judged my son for I did. I went to the Lord very upset about the damage. I felt like such a fool. He said,

Son,

You must start by forgiving your son for his carelessness, but you have reaped what you have sown. You judged him as careless, and you were careless. Son, repent and forgive, and although it will not repair the TV, the small scratch will always remind you not to judge and not to hold onto any unforgiveness. Consider this to be a grace event. If you have learned never to judge as a result of the price of a TV, it is a small price to pay. Now come to me when you worry about your stuff and ask me to protect it. Forgive your kids, and expect them to respect and protect your things. Now rest in this lesson. Yes, it is painful, but it will pass and the sweet fruit of discipline will be forever manifested in your life.

During this time of discipline, I saw the Lord look right at me, and I saw His lips move as He led me through prayers of forgiveness and inner healing.

At times the Lord has exhorted me in dreams. Exhortation is different than discipline; it is a strong word of encouragement that if not followed could have disastrous results. Once I dreamed that I had accepted the lead role in the play *Macbeth*, which is a Shakespearian play written in old English. I did not know the play, but I felt confident that I could do it.

On the day of the play, I arrived at the theatre late. After I got into my costume, the director gave me a cheque for $500. It was only then that I realized I did not know the play. I had not learned my lines, I had not practiced the part, and I could not even read the play because the old English words were unfamiliar to me. I woke up, and I asked the Lord, "What does the dream mean?" He said,

Son,

This is a prophetic warning to always understand and practice your seminars before you do them. If you do not, you will lose your reputation as a competent speaker. You must understand them well. It is your reputation on the line, not anyone else's. Never let others dictate to you to say their presentation, but always write your own, know the material, and practice it before speaking on the topic.

Love, Dad.

This dream and the interpretation were particularly relevant to me that week. My company had given me eight new seminars to deliver. I was also expected to coach the entire Canadian sales force on how to deliver these seminars. There was pressure to deliver the seminars in the way they were written, but that would not have been a good idea because they did not communicate the value of the products and services in a way I was comfortable with. Because of the dream, I spent a great deal of time learning this new material and writing my own seminars and felt confident when I presented them. As a result, I was able to coach the sales force much more effectively.

The Lord wants us to live a life of peace and joy; however, our mistakes can often rob us of that result. God wants to correct us and help us to see our mistakes and deal with them. He will often speak to us about them if we listen. Have you ever felt a sense of uneasiness, a sense of conviction that you have done something wrong? This is often God trying to get our attention. In this personal action plan, I encourage you to be honest with God about these feelings and ask Him to speak to you about them.

Personal Action

1. Write out any sense of uneasiness or feeling that you have done something wrong.

2. Focus the eyes of your heart on the Lord and discuss your feelings with Him. Ask Him, "Why do I feel like this? What should I do to be free from these feelings?"

3. Write down what the Lord says about this. Sins are very personal, and therefore I recommend that you use codes to describe specific sins. In this way, you are protected if anyone reads your journals.

4. I encourage you to repent of anything the Lord shows you.

CHAPTER FOURTEEN

Conclusion

This book is a personal account of my journey with the Lord, of my secret place. I don't know where the secret place is, but when I lead worship I often look there. I see Jesus there, and although I am leading worship in the physical realm, I am often worshipping in the Heavenly realm at the same time. I now often stand in both realms at the same time. Once while I was leading worship, I saw angels come down in front of the cottage. Some were carrying lawn chairs. They were talking together, and they were dressed in different clothes. As I started to lead worship in the physical realm, they all joined in and sang and danced with us.

My secret place is not likely to be the same as yours. Do not seek a place like I have. Focus your eyes on the author and perfector of your faith, Jesus, not on a physical place. If He wishes to show you more, let Him, but don't look for that. However do not be surprised if He does expand the vision as He did for me. When He was on the earth, He used parables to illustrate a truth and to help us understand His kingdom better. I have found that many of the places the Lord has taken me to in my secret place have reinforced a specific truth He wanted to tell me, much like He used the parables.

Over the last 18 years I have recorded thousands of words I have heard from the Lord. In this book I have described only a few of my experiences with Him. Faith and wisdom come from His spoken word. I have found wisdom is developed over time as He weaves His written and spoken word together with real-life situations. It takes time to understand His wisdom, and I have found that it is in the secret place, where there is only you and the Lord, that wisdom grows and is applied to our lives.

In closing, let me leave you with one last thought. The overall test of what we hear and experience is God's peace in our heart. Sometimes the experiences the Lord will take us through are painful; sometimes they are meant to discipline us. However, His peace is the overall final test, and we need to let it rule in our hearts. My hope is that as a result of this book, you will be encouraged to know the Lord more intimately and to develop a deeper relationship with Him in your very own secret place.

Love,
Bill

How to Hear God's Voice

Hearing from God is easy. Since you are reading this section, you may not quite believe that. To begin, we need to embrace one simple truth: God wants to speak to you.

Some are afraid to look for a spiritual answer from God—afraid that they are not worthy, afraid of what He might say, afraid He will punish them. The truth is God is big. Jesus said, *"If [your child] asks for a fish, will [you] give him a snake? If you, then, though you are evil, know how to give good gifts to your children, how much more will your Father in heaven give good gifts to those who ask him!"*[28] He is inviting us to ask Him. Others are afraid they will be deceived. I encourage you to have more faith that God can speak to you than the devil has power to deceive you. We must believe that God will speak to us.

The process of hearing from God is described in the Bible. King David, the prophets, Jesus, and the apostles all heard from God very clearly and lived in a state of constant communication with their Heavenly Father. The setting for hearing God did differ from person to person. Jesus would draw away from the crowd where He could be alone. King David used to go to the temple and sit before the Lord. Elisha called for a minstrel to play so he could hear from God. Although in different settings, they all used the same four steps to hear from God. These steps were:

1. They recognised that God speaks to us in our mind, in our thoughts.
2. They chose to hear, to listen, to see, and would draw away and become quiet.

3. They would focus the eyes of their hearts on the Lord, look for vision and listen to His flow of thoughts.
4. They would write down what they saw or heard so it could be shared with others.

God speaks to us in our thoughts. These thoughts may be words or images; however, this is not the only way God speaks to us. Just as we have five physical senses, we have five spiritual senses, and God can speak to us using any of those senses. For the sake of learning how to hear God, we will start with the basics and look at the Biblical accounts of how King David and the prophet Habakkuk heard from God.

King David provides us with an excellent example of how he heard from God. He asked God about building His temple, and God gave Him very specific directions. Let's look at how he heard God.

King David rose to his feet and said: "Listen to me, my brothers and my people. I had it in my heart to build a house as a place of rest for the ark of the covenant of the LORD...Then David gave his son Solomon the plans for the portico of the temple, its buildings, its storerooms, its upper parts, its inner rooms and the place of atonement. He gave him the plans of all that the Spirit had put in his mind for the courts of the temple of the LORD and all the surrounding rooms, for the treasuries of the temple of God and for the treasuries for the dedicated things. He gave him instructions for the divisions of the priests and Levites, and for all the work of serving in the temple of the LORD, as well as for all the articles to be used in its service. He designated the weight of gold for all the gold articles to be used in various kinds of service, and the weight of silver for all the silver articles to be used in various kinds of service...He also gave him the plan for the chariot, that is, the cherubim of gold that spread their wings and shelter the ark of the covenant of the LORD. "All this," David said, "I have in writing from the hand of the LORD upon me, and he gave me understanding in all the details of the plan."[29]

We can see the four steps that David followed to hear God.

1. David knew God spoke to him in his mind.

2. David decided to inquire of the Lord about building the temple and quieted his heart before Him.

3. David tuned into the flow of God's voice, and the Lord began to speak to him. The Lord put the thoughts in David's mind. He told David how the temple should be built. He described how it should be organized, what it should look like, and how much gold and silver should be used for each item in the temple.

4. David wrote down what the Lord showed him, and he gave it to his son Solomon to build.

As I read David's account of this experience, I am amazed at the level of detail in the revelation the Lord gave him. The plans were precise and all encompassing. The process was not complex. King David simply asked God, heard God in his mind tell him what he was to do, and wrote it down.

I wanted to learn how to do that, to hear God's plans for me. I went to a man who prophesied in a church. When I asked him how he knew God was speaking to him, he told me that he "just knew in his knower." I thought, *You're a big help.* I never did figure out how to hear God from him. Yet King David's approach was so simple. He just shared his heart with God, and God gave him specific thoughts in his mind. What could be easier? I could do that.

The prophet Habakkuk also heard from God the way King David did. Habakkuk recorded his experience. He said:

"I will stand at my watch and station myself on the ramparts; I will look to see what he will say to me, and what answer I am to give to this complaint. Then the LORD replied: 'Write down the revelation and make it plain on tablets so that a herald may run with it.'"[30]

Again I could see the four steps.

1. Habakkuk knew God spoke to him in his mind.

2. Habakkuk chose to hear from God and drew himself away to a place of solitude. He would go up the defensive wall (his watch) around his town to listen to God. This is such an important first step. We have to be quiet to hear God. He doesn't yell at us. He speaks to us in a quiet voice in our mind.

3. Habakkuk looked to see what God was saying. God speaks to us in both words and pictures; He will often give us images because it is faster. The saying "a picture is worth a thousand words" is so true. Habakkuk tuned into a flow of thoughts and images (the revelation) that were in his mind.

4. Habakkuk wrote them down.

I have found that God is not in a hurry and that He will speak slowly enough for me to write down what He is saying. Sometimes He only gives me one word at a time so I can write it down while He is speaking.

Jesus said we must become as little children to enter His kingdom. Little children are quite different from older children. Little children believe what their father says, they believe that their father knows everything, and they believe he can do everything. Little children find it easy to use their imagination when Mom or Dad read stories to them. For us to enter the kingdom of God and consistently hear from God, we have to step back and retrieve these beliefs and abilities in our lives.

Some believe that any use of their imagination to focus the eyes of their heart on the Lord is wrong, possibly new age or even idolatry. In the Hebrew language, the word *meditate* includes the meaning to imagine. We need to discard the false belief that we cannot use our imagination when we meditate on the Lord. We need to acknowledge that everything God made is good and God can use that part of our mind to communicate with us.

Some believe that God doesn't talk directly to people anymore. They believe that this type of communication passed away with the apostles. This is not true, God has not changed. He loves to communicate with us His children, and we need to break agreement with this false belief as well.

Personal Action

The truth is, God wants to talk to you and He has made it easy to do it. Let's start by learning how to listen for the voice of God.

Most of us have experienced having a song on our heart, and we find ourselves singing or humming along with the song. Try singing the song "Happy Birthday" in your mind.

When you can do this, check this box. ❏

Happy Birthday to You
Happy Birthday to You
Happy Birthday, Happy Birthday
Happy Birthday to You

Keep doing this until you are able to do it easily. This is the place in our mind where God speaks to us. God speaks to us as a stream of thoughts.

It is often said that children have a vivid imagination. When you were a child, did you imagine the story your mom or dad read to you? I remember my mother reading me the novel *Mysterious Island* by Jules Verne. Each lunch hour when I came home from school, she would read a chapter to me. I loved it. I could envision Captain Nemo and the Nautilus and the giant creatures that were in the story.

God also uses visions when he speaks to us. Visions are simply images that He gives us. He often uses images because a lot of information can be conveyed with a simple picture. To start seeing visions, you have to know where to look. In your mind, there is an imagination screen. We use this screen when we imagine images and scenes. We use our mind to create the images. When God gives us a vision, He uses this same screen. The difference is that He is the one who paints the picture and our mind is not involved.

Let's do an exercise to practice using your imagination screen. I want you to imagine your home. Check off the box when you can see each scene.

1. Imagine the home you live in. ❏
2. Walk through the front door. ❏
3. Go into the kitchen. ❏
4. Open the fridge. ❏

5. Find the apples.   ❑
6. Choose a green one.   ❑
7. Bite into the apple.   ❑

You have just used your imagination screen. This ability was given to us by God so we can bring new ideas into being. At first you may find it difficult to imagine in colour, but keep at it and it will get easier.

Now that we know where to look and listen, let's try hearing from God. To start, we will focus the eyes of our hearts on the author of our faith, Jesus. We do this by simply imagining a Bible story. Children love to imagine a story. I would like you to become like a little child and just imagine this paraphrased story of Jesus and His disciples (John 21).

Jesus looked over the Sea of Galilee. He stood up on a grassy hill where the onshore breeze blew over the grass and caught His white robe and hair. He wanted to meet His disciples, who had gone out fishing that morning. Jesus knew that they had had a rough couple of days, so He planned to prepare breakfast for them. He had some fish and bread and walked down along the beach. You could hear the waves lapping against the shore. He built a small fire, cooked the fish, and was warming himself while he waited for His disciples to return.

As the disciples drew close to the shore, they could see a man on the beach but they did not recognize who he was. Jesus called to them and said, "Did you catch any fish?"

They replied, "No we did not."

He called to them and said, "Let down your nets on the other side of your boat." The disciples did just as they were told and a large number of fish jumped into the net. The water was alive with fish. The sun reflected off their scales, and the water was shaking violently as the fish fought to get into the net. Nathaniel looked at Peter with astonishment. The disciples had caught so many fish they could not pull the net into the boat.

Peter looked from the fish to the man on the beach. John said, "It is the Lord." Peter wrapped himself in his robe, jumped into the water, and swam towards the beach. Peter ran up to Jesus and fell on his face at His feet. Jesus saw him and began to speak to him. After a few moments, Peter went to help the other disciples bring in the net of fish and Jesus went back and sat by the fire.

1. Now go and sit down beside Jesus at the fire and look at him right in the face. Spend some time looking at Him. After a few moments of looking at Him, ask Him this question, "Do you love me?"

2. Write down what Jesus says or does.

You have just heard from the Lord. I gave you a question to which there is only one answer, "Yes." However, what I want you to experience is how the Lord says yes to you. In most cases it is very personal.

The story you imagined was used to focus your eyes on the Lord and on the written word of God. It was used to help you to make the transition from the written word of God to the spoken word of God. Let's do some more hearing and seeing.

3. Now go back to the scene of Jesus sitting at the fire and look at Him again. Ask Him, "Please tell me more."

4. Write down what Jesus says or does.

You have just heard from God. You have followed the four steps.

1. You recognised God speaks to you in your mind.
2. You quieted your heart by imagining the Bible story.
3. You focused the eyes and ears of your heart on the Lord and you tuned into the flow of thoughts that come from God.
4. You wrote it down.

Jesus wants to meet with you face to face. He is not restricted by time or space. He will meet with you in your mind since according to King David, this is the realm of spiritual connection.

Let's do one final exercise. Please go back to where you saw Jesus by the fire and look at Him again.

5. Ask Him this question: "What would You like to say to me today?"

6. Write down what Jesus says or does.

7. Call a friend and tell them you are practicing hearing from God. Describe what you heard Jesus say or do and ask them if it sounds like God to them.

After we have written down what God says, we can test it to ensure that it is God's word. There are several tests we can do.

1. First, we test it against the Bible. God will not contradict His written word.
2. Second, we test it against the characteristics of our Heavenly Father: God is love, God is kind, God is merciful. God will not say things that are harsh, mean-spirited, or cynical. All true prophetic words build up, encourage, and comfort.
3. Third, we test it against the names of God. God will not contradict His own names. Here are some of the names of God:

* Jehovah Elohim—The Lord Is God
* Jehovah Nissi—The Lord Is My Banner
* Jehovah Rophi—The Lord Who Heals Me
* Jehovah Jireh—The Lord Who Provides
* Jehovah Tzadekenu—The Lord Our Righteousness
* Jehovah Shalom—The Lord of Peace
* Jehovah Rohi—The Lord Is My Shepherd
* Jehovah Shammah—The Lord Is Here

4. We test it with others. The body of Christ will witness to true words. There is great safety when you are accountable to someone else who will give you their honest opinion.

Now that you have heard God's voice I invite you to return to the book and continue your journey with Him. Take this opportunity to talk with Him and hear His will for your life.

For additional information on how to hear God's voice
or to learn how to be counselled by God,
please contact Communion with God Ministries

www.cwgministries.org
CWG Fulfillment Center, 3792 Broadway St., Buffalo, NY 14227
Email: mark@cluonline.com
Phone: 1-800-466-6961 or 716-681-4896
Fax: 716-685-3908

Endnotes

[1] Psalm 91:1 KJV

[2] John 10:27 NIV

[3] Psalm 91:1 KJV

[4] Romans 5:8 NIV

[5] Mark 12:30 NIV

[6] Psalm 37:4 NIV

[7] Wikipedia

[8] James 1:5 NIV

[9] Hebrews 12:22-24 NIV

[10] Psalm 34:7 NIV

[11] www.youtube.com "Reclaim 7 Mountains of Culture"

[12] Philippians 4:6 NIV

[13] Romans 10:17 NIV

[14] 2 Corinthians 10:5 NIV

[15] Philippians 4:6-7

[16] John 14:6 NIV

[17] Mark 14:36 NIV

[18] John 14:26 NIV

[19] Matthew 16:19 NIV

[20] Nehemiah 1:11 NIV

[21] Matthew 5:16 KJV

22 www.acdi-cida.gc.ca

23 Matthew 7:7 NIV

24 Proverbs 24:6 KJV

25 Colossians 3:15 NIV

26 Proverbs 3:11-12 NIV

27 Matthew 7:1-2 NIV

28 Matthew 7:10-11 NIV

29 1 Chronicles 28:2,11-13,18,19 NIV

30 Habakkuk 2:1-2 NIV

AUTHOR BIOGRAPHY

Bill and Susan Dupley

Bill and Sue have been ministering for over 25 years, preaching and leading worship on five continents. Together they minister renewal and teach adults and children how to hear the voice of God. Bill and Sue believe that the supernatural should be the natural for all believers and that every believer can impact their world for the kingdom of God as they hear God's will and follow His leading.

Bill and Sue's home church is Catch the Fire Toronto where they lead worship and have been ministering the "Toronto Blessing" to God's family. Together they have co-authored "Kids in Renewal," a dynamic Sunday school program published by Strang Publishing that teaches children their Heavenly Father's heart for them, how to hear His voice, and how to receive and impart spiritual gifts.

Bill and Sue are certified facilitators for Communion with God Ministries and have conducted seminars at Catch the Fire, Mission Fest, Releasers of Life, Iris Ministries, and many other churches in North America, Africa, Australia, Europe, and Asia. Their passion is for God's family to know their Heavenly Father and to hear His voice, so that they may live in the fullness of the gifts and the freedom that Jesus bought for them.

Bill and Sue came to the Lord in 1976. Since that time, the Lord has guided them through business careers, and they have experienced the blessing of the Lord in their business and ministry.

Bill is currently the Canadian Chief Solutions Manager for a global technology company, and Susan is a nurse in a Canadian community college's health centre. Susan is a graduate of the University of Toronto in Nursing Science, and Bill is a graduate of Ryerson University in Electronics Technology. Bill and Sue are affiliated with Catch the Fire and Communion with God Ministries.

Notes